STRAIGHT
THINKING
ABOUT
GOD

by Ord L. Morrow
Associate Radio Minister
Back to the Bible Broadcast

D1408057

Back to the Bible
Lincoln, Nebraska 68501

85,000 printed to date—1976
(5-5337—85M—36)
ISBN 0-8474-0711-X

Printed in the United States of America

Contents

Chapter 1

A Biblical Concept of God

If my ears are not playing tricks on me, something is terribly wrong in our world. I have been listening for many years to the testimonies of those who believe in one God, who is the Father of the Lord Jesus Christ.

Across the years I have heard thousands speak concerning their relationships with God and His Son. Every time I have heard them, without one single exception, they have said that being a Christian is the most amazing, the most wonderful thing that can possibly happen to a human being. I am aware that we can speak one thing and live another. It is always possible to tell a half-truth. But as I listen to them, I am impressed that they are honestly and sincerely trying to convey to any who will listen the worth and the wealth of knowing God through His Son, Jesus Christ. They search for the most expressive words they can find to tell of their joy.

If you move back a few years, you will hear them say, "To know God, to receive Jesus Christ as Lord and Saviour, is just great. It is wonderful! It is rich and rewarding. It is blessed beyond belief! It is satisfying and sure." There is no end to their praise of the position they now possess in Christ.

The "now generation," expressing the same satisfaction, may use words like "It's the greatest happening of my life; it's cool, groovy and right on, and this is the One Way."

Admitting there have been some bad apples in the bucket, still you cannot deny that the universal testimony of those who have found Christ is one of assurance, joy, peace and satisfaction. I hear this, and I am happy! But I am haunted by a question: If all these testimonies are true, and I'm sure they are, why is it that everyone does not seek the same thing, trust in the same Lord and find the same joy?

When I turn to those who have never professed to know God, I find that the puzzle deepens. History records very few times with as much unhappiness and as much personal tension as we possess today. While this is no place to quote the statistics on crime, divorce, immorality and mental collapse, the testimony of the average man is that something is missing in his life. He sees no peace in the world, he does not know peace in his heart, and most likely there is very little peace in his home. To him joy is a word, a sound. It is not that he does not try to be joyful; he works at it most of the time. The fact is, however, that the wells from which he drinks do not produce any sense of deep joy. In his effort to find meaning he may set a goal in life, yet he is not sure he wants to reach the goal. He fears that when he does, he will join a number of his friends who reached their goal only to be disappointed and even discouraged with life.

What comes after position or power or wealth? Where does one go from there? Or what does one do with power and position so he may have worth, meaning and purpose in life? Do these things in themselves give a man that knowledge, feeling and assurance of real wealth and worth in the world? What is Mr. Average Man's hope? He hopes he will be well. He hopes to make a good living for his family. He hopes to retire early. He hopes to play a bit with the grandchildren. But beyond that his life and purpose are blanks. What does he hope for out of life? What hope does he have for his family? What hope does he have for his grandchildren? What is his hope after this life? He is not sure!

There is a frantic search in our times for reality, a search for identity. Our age asks almost in fright, "Who am I?" Why all this panic? Have they not heard the testimonies of those who said they had found reality and more in Christ? Have they not heard a thousand voices saying that in Christ the search for reality and identity ends?

The mystery of all this deepens when you remember that there is a mysterious longing in the heart of every person. We are never sure how to express this longing. We call it "a search for life." Youth cries, "I want to live!" Age looks on wondering, having lived a number of years, yet not sure what youth really means.

There is a longing for love. We were made with the need to love and to be loved. Yet the evidence indicates that we experience more hate than love. In our desperate longing for love, we have even mixed it with lust, thinking—tragic blunder—that love and lust are the same.

Sometimes the cry of the empty heart is for reality. Things do not seem real. We go through life feeling like a person walking underwater. Everything is out of focus, unreal to sight, sound and touch. If only we could find reality; if only things would clear up!

But the Christian has said clearly, urgently, earnestly and forcefully, over and over, that our search for life, love and reality ends with Jesus Christ! He is all this and more. So why do wealth and want, joy and joylessness exist together? Why does not everyone find the life, the love, the hope, the assurance of worth, the reality he so desperately wants? In other words, why do so few confess Jesus Christ as Lord, since He is the One who gives eternal life? And this life is not a quality of life that just runs on and on; it is a quality of life which brings to the heart that final sigh of eternal rest, knowing it has finally reached its destiny. Why do so few come to what the Bible calls "salvation"?

The answer is found in the Scriptures themselves. Reading the Scripture with even one eye open, it becomes obvious that many would be saved if they knew their danger. We talk much of reality, but we are not actually realists at all. Truth may be hard to find, but it is much harder to face. The fact that danger exists does not mean that we realize our danger—far from it! The Devil is certainly no dope, and he keeps us so busy and tired or keeps our minds so occupied with things which do not matter that we do not have time to think of things as they are. We cannot blame the Devil for everything, but he certainly has his finger in the pie of our maddening busyness.

8

We are running scared, but we do not have time to think or the moral courage to admit that we are running scared! In fact, if you were to tell Mr. Average Man he was in danger, you would get a look which would clearly say, "Danger? What danger? I'm in no danger at all."

Humans have always been that way. It was true in the days of the flood. Noah was a "preacher of righteousness" (II Pet. 2:5). The evidence seems to indicate that it took about 120 years for the building of the ark (see Gen. 6:3). As Noah preached righteousness, he must have mentioned the danger that was coming. If he didn't say it in words, he certainly said it by building the ark! Somebody surely asked him why he was building such a contraption.

Of course, we were not there, and we have no record (except that they were ungodly), but their response, since they were as human as we are, must have been something like this: "Danger? A judgment coming? That just shows you what religion does to a fellow's mind! Doesn't he know anything about the goodness of man? Has he never heard of the love of God? Poor old man; he has lost touch with his times. He is suffering delusions; he's out of his head!" But they were in danger even if they did not recognize it or admit it. Facts do not change simply because we do not believe them.

Our danger, of course, is not from a flood. Our immediate danger may not be in the form of a judgment of God, although the judgment for sin is more sure than the setting of the sun. Our present danger, at least one of them, is our poor concept of God. We do not know the God of all the earth, the maker of heaven and earth. We have little concept of His character, what He is like. We know practically nothing of what He will do, how He will act under certain circumstances. We have our opinions, but our words and our deeds eloquently deny that we know the one true God.

"The Lord is in his holy temple," cries the prophet, "let all the earth keep silence before him" (Hab. 2:20). Silence? In a frantic world like ours? Ours is a world of clanging cymbals, of beating drums, of crashing instruments, of songs screamed into a turned-up microphone. No! The god we know is a god of noise.

Because we have lost any biblical concept of God, we invent our own ideas about Him. We cannot conceive that the God revealed in the Old Testament has any real relationship to the Jesus Christ of the New Testament. Jesus Christ is not, in the minds of most, high, holy, mighty or divine. To most He is not now, and never can be, a judge; that is unthinkable. To them He is meek and mild and is surely upset over some of the things God did in the Old Testament.

Most of us know the god we want to know. We make him fit our image of God; he is a big brother—smiling, indulgent and impotent. The god we have invented is entirely soft; he can be kind, loving and forgiving—nothing else. He must let us have our way; he must not cross us, change us, convict us or condemn us. We might allow him to have a friendly chat with us about our weaknesses but nothing more. The god we have invented must never surprise us or frighten us. We have him measured; he can be managed, controlled, quieted. He must be, at most, a tolerant observer of our sins and be ready at a moment's notice to get us out of any trouble.

Therein lies our danger—we can manage and manipulate our god. The god of the average person has no power to command, no absolutes to govern and no rights to impose. When the God of the Bible passed by Eliphaz, the hair of his flesh stood up (Job 4:15). Our god would not dare to mess up our hair! When the God of the Bible spoke to Daniel, he became so weak he had to have divine strengthening merely to stand (Dan. 10:8,9,18). But our god may not make us bow even our knees. When Isaiah saw the God of the Bible, He was "high and lifted up" (Isa. 6:1). His train filled the temple; one seraph cried out to another, "Holy, holy, holy, is the Lord of hosts: the whole earth is full of his glory" (v. 3). Our modern, plastic god has no temple, nobody speaks of him as holy and no one fears him.

Our danger is real. When we lose God, we have lost all. What do we know of a God who appeared to Paul, who then fell into the dust, trembling and astonished? Paul asked, "Who art thou, Lord? And the Lord said, I am Jesus whom thou persecutest" (Acts 9:5). Stewart was entirely right when he said, "The first reaction of a real religious experience is quite devastatingly humiliating."

Our danger comes from the fact that we do not know God. To see God with understanding is to see, perhaps for the first time, ourselves. It is to shift the center back where it belongs—from man to God.

To see how real our danger is, one need but think a moment of what we have done with the anger of God. What a strange thought for our

11

times—God, angry! But the Bible has more to say of God's wrath than of His love. Jesus talked more of hell that He did of heaven. But when we hear these things, we get nervous. We are not used to a God who has a reason or a right to be angry.

The expression "wrath of God" occurs 10 times in the New Testament. Add to these the other passages that speak of God's wrath, and you have more than 40 occurences in the New Testament alone.

In the Old Testament God spoke through His prophet Hosea: "I will pour out my wrath . . . like water" (Hos. 5:10) and through Zephaniah: "For my determination is to gather the nations, that I may assemble the kingdoms, to pour upon them mine indignation, even all my fierce anger" (Zeph. 3:8).

From the New Testament we learn that "the wrath of God is revealed from heaven against all ungodliness and unrighteousness" (Rom. 1:18). The standard of righteousness is God's Word alone, not any law of any land! And again, "Unto them that . . . do not obey the truth, . . . indignation and wrath, tribulation and anguish" (2:8,9). After reading Ephesians 5:6, you would think Paul had a peek at our times: "Because of these things cometh the wrath of God upon the children of disobedience." What things? "Fornication, and all uncleanness, . . . covetousness, . . . filthiness, . . . foolish talking, . . . jesting" (vv. 3,4).

Our warped concept of God is our danger. When we think of God's being angry, we are somewhat shocked. We forget that God's anger is not an outburst of passion but rather His holy will against sin. He is not angry because He wants to be angry but because He must be in order to retain His holiness. If we are to be saved, we must see God as He is, not as we might wish He were or dream that He is.

We are comfortable with a Lord Jesus who drives demons from men (Mark 5), and we give three cheers for demonic deliverance; but we are not so comfortable with a Lord Jesus who drives men from the temple (John 2). We are comfortable with a God who loves, but we are decidedly uncomfortable with a God who laughs when love is spurned (Ps. 2). The God of the Bible can give life, and He can take it away; and He does.

The rich man in Luke 16:19-31 did not think he was in any danger. He knew life was sweet, but he did not know it was short! Our low view of God has brought us near spiritual, moral and social bankruptcy. When will we see once more the "goodness and severity of God"? (Rom. 11:22). When will we believe God's full revelation of Himself, humble ourselves and cry, "Depth of mercy, can there be, Mercy still reserved for me? / Can my God His wrath forbear? Me, the chief of sinners spare?" The answer is a clear "Yes, He can." For as God has said, He delights in mercy and is not willing that any should perish (Mic. 7:18; II Pet. 3:9). But before we are ever to know the mercy, the grace, the love of God, we will need to destroy our human concepts and get back to biblical concepts of God, which will put us—and God—where we belong!

Chapter 2

A Poor Concept of Sin

We have said that our first danger comes from a poor concept of God. Every danger we face is related to this first one. If our concept of God is right, all will go fairly well; if our concept of God is wrong, nothing can be right.

Our second danger, then, may very well be our poor concept of sin. If we have no fear of God, we are certainly not going to have any fear of sin. In fact, our concept of sin is in such a state of decay that the person who seems afraid of sin is considered somewhat odd! This fact in itself should warn us that we are in imminent danger. Our opinions on the important subject of sin do not mean much. We must know what God has said.

The Bible makes it clear that in his natural state, man is a sinner—one who has broken God's law, rebelled at His Word and refused His will. Ephesians 2:1 states it: "Dead in trespasses and sins." There must be no confusion here. Our condition must be set forth so clearly that no question can remain as to guilt and who is guilty. Romans 3:10,23 says, "There is none righteous, no, not one. . . . For all have sinned, and come short of the glory of God." This is our condition, whether or

15

not we feel it, know it, admit it, believe it or deny it. Thus we will, man by man, collect the wages of our sin, and the wages of sin is death (6:23).

Our danger is that we simply will not accept God's estimate of us, and we will not accept that which is everywhere evident—death is universal. We fit the wise man's description: "Because sentence against an evil work is not executed speedily, therefore the heart of the sons of men is fully set in them to do evil" (Eccles. 8:11). We are alive, aren't we? Death is a long way off, isn't it? To reason in this way is to miss the meaning of both sin and death. We are not about to die, we are dead already. The sentence on Adam was "Thou shalt surely die" (Gen. 2:17). He was a dying man the minute he disobeyed. Death is not a ceasing of existence, it is a condition of separation from God. We are not to be separated sometime in the future; we are separated now.

Look at the word of the Lord Jesus concerning this: "He that believeth not the Son [of God] shall not see life; but the wrath of God abideth on him" (John 3:36). In one sense, our separation from God is not final until we die physically, but we are separated from Him now.

There is no clearer word on the matter than Isaiah 59: "Behold, the Lord's hand is not so short that it cannot save; neither is His ear so dull that it cannot hear. But your iniquities [sins] have made a separation between you and your God, and your sins have hid His face from you, so that He does not hear. For your hands are defiled with blood, and your fingers with iniquity; your lips have spoken falsehood, your tongue mutters wickedness. No one sues righteously and no one pleads

16

honestly. They trust in confusion, and speak lies; they conceive mischief, and bring forth iniquity. . . . An act of violence is in their hands. Their feet run to evil, and they hasten to shed innocent blood; their thoughts are thoughts of iniquity. . . . They do not know the way of peace, and there is no justice in their tracks; they have made their paths crooked; whoever treads on them does not know peace.

"Therefore, justice is far from us, and righteousness does not overtake us; we hope for light, but behold, darkness; for brightness, but we walk in gloom. We grope along the wall like blind men, we grope like those who have no eyes; we stumble at midday as in the twilight, among those who are vigorous we are like dead men. All of us growl like bears, and moan sadly like doves; we hope for justice, but there is none, for salvation, but it is far from us. For our transgressions are multiplied before Thee, and our sins testify against us; for our transgressions are with us, and we know our iniquities" (vv. 1-4,6-12, NASB).

Had we read such a piece of literature without knowing its source, we might well surmise that it was in today's newspaper! Our danger is that we do not know the condemnation of sin. We think we can play with fire and never get burned. We somehow think God does not see or care or is unable to do anything about wickedness anyway! We have, from our warped concept of sin, concluded that man is not a sinner. We excuse what we are and what we do. Sin becomes a sickness, a weakness, something that is not our fault. It is the fault of parents who did not give us enough love, of circumstances which allowed us to be born in

17

unfortunate surroundings, of health, of misunder-
standings or of the surrounding society which
pressured us into the mold to which we now conform. What we do just cannot be our fault.

If we cannot dodge our responsibility, then we
swing to the other extreme and say, "But I have
my rights! Who has a right to tell me what is right
or wrong for me?" We want to consult a computer
or take a vote on what is and what is not sin. We
want to set our own life-style. If we want to
change partners every full moon, that is our
business. But all of these ideas and excuses miss the
point. We are not sinners because we sin; we sin
because we are sinners. We do what we do because
we are what we are.

The smell of death is upon us. We are cut off
from life. If we want to change our ways, we will
have to change our lives, from the inside out. We
fail to take sin seriously because we do not realize
that it is the basic cause of our suffering, misery,
pain and heartache. Admitting that we are sinners
by nature in our actions and in our standing before
God is no easy pill for us to swallow. Therein is the
danger; thus, we either take our medicine or die!

A casual skip through the Scriptures reveals
that we are the servants of sin (John 8:34); death
entered because of sin (Rom. 5:12); that which is
not of faith is sin (14:23); the sting of death is
sin (I Cor. 15:56); sin is deceitful and hardens our
hearts (Heb. 3:13); sin easily besets us, clings to us
and entangles us (12:1); to him that knows to do
good and does not do it, it is sin (James 4:17). No
wonder Proverbs 14:9 says, "Fools make a mock at
sin." We are assured in Numbers 32:23: "Be sure
your sin will find you out."

18

When we consider sin, we easily forget that if we name sin by another name or miscalculate its effects or rob it of its real character, then we have taken away our need for any restitution, redemption or salvation. We may like to rob sin of its sting, but can we? What shall we do with the fact of guilt?

We may say that modern man is not a sinner and needs no outside help. But look at the evidence. We do not fight because of our love for one another, we do not drug ourselves because we are filled with joy, we do not cheat out of deep concern for our brother, our fears do not overwhelm us from a sense of quiet! We are not a nation that takes tons and tons of tranquilizers and other pills every day because we are so happy!

If sin is not the problem, then what is? What is the trouble with us, where is the defect that makes us creatures of such horror and evil? What did happen to our personalities that caused them to disintegrate and degenerate until we can, and do, act like beasts? Of course, some answer that we are beasts—nothing more! Then war is due to the survival of those animal instincts we inherited from our beast grandparents.

But if this is true, when is the animal part to die so that we can begin to act like human beings? We have been living, or trying to live, in some sort of civilized existence for at least 6000 years, and these so-called animal instincts are not decreasing but increasing. Do we imagine that we can give a person a new electric can opener, a new car and a thick carpet on his floor and change his nature? To say our problem is a hangover of animal instincts offers no solution and gives no answers to the main issue of what is wrong with man.

It would be nice—we think—if we could so easily settle our two problems—what to do with God and what to do with sin. One thing is certain—you either have to rid man of a holy God to whom he is responsible or you must acknowledge him to be a sinner. Our first danger is that we do not know God, and our second is like it—we have lost our concept of sin. When you say the word "sin," you say, at the same time, three things. First, man is a creation of God, made in His image. God gave man a will as a part of his personality. Second, man violated the known will of God; he became guilty. He chose a path, a way contrary to God. Third, man is in a condition of death, a condition from which he cannot rescue himself.

But before we become discouraged beyond measure, we need to ask, Is there no cure for sin? That is the whole point of the gospel! Of course there is a cure for it. The trouble is that we will not recognize our disease! All that I have said about sin is meant to bring us to the point of admitting our need. The whole point of saying that a poor concept of sin is a danger is to make us realize that if we lose our concept of sin, we lose our sense of need!

If this were not happening to us right and left, there would be no need for us to talk about such a danger. But it is happening. It is serious. If we cut off or deny the knowledge of sin or refuse to admit our failure, then nothing is left for the Holy Spirit to use as a handle for conviction! Without conviction we are lost!

Confession does not save us, but it is a first step in the right direction. Confession does not cleanse us, but it makes us aware of our need of cleansing. Saving from the penalty of sin, from its horrible power, from its guilt, from its condemnation, is the whole message of the gospel. "Christ died for our sins according to the scriptures" (I Cor. 15:3).

We must make the gospel clear at this point, just in case someone might be overcome with the knowledge of sin or with the feeling of guilt and throw up his hands and say, "No hope for me!" Yes, there is hope! Death reigns in Adam, but life reigns in Christ. What we need as a first step is simply to admit our sin—for remember, "He that covereth his sins shall not prosper" (Prov. 28:13)—confess it, throw ourselves on the mercy and the grace of God and receive the Saviour! You will never have to look for an excuse again! You will never have to find an excuse for what you have done or what you are. "Sin shall not have dominion over you" (Rom. 6:14). "Being then made free from sin" (v. 18). "For the wages of sin is death; but the gift of God is eternal life through Jesus Christ our Lord" (v. 23).

Chapter 3

A Poor Concept of Jesus Christ

We have dealt with the danger we encounter when we have a poor, or warped, concept of God and of sin. It then follows almost logically that our next danger might well come from our poor concept of Jesus Christ. Anything short of a biblical concept is bound to be out of focus.

Opinions abound concerning Jesus Christ. Some will say He was a fine man, a good man and even a fine teacher. Some will say He was a revolutionary, a radical fighting the establishment. Some say that He was a misguided prophet trying to effect change for which His times were not ready, and that was what nailed Him to the cross.

When it comes to any realistic concept concerning Jesus, opinions are about as numerous as the sands of the sea and just as worthless! We must have more than man's opinions; we must have the revelation of God concerning Him.

To find an answer, we ask, What was His work? What was the purpose of His being here? He came, the Scriptures say, to bring man and God together in peace. He was to be a man, a last Adam (I Cor. 15:45), so that He could represent man honestly before God.

"Forasmuch then as the children are partakers of flesh and blood, he also himself likewise took part of the same; that through death he might destroy him that had the power of death, that is, the devil; and deliver them who through fear of death were all their lifetime subject to bondage. For verily he took not on him the nature of angels; but he took on him the seed of Abraham. Wherefore in all things it behoved him to be made like unto his brethren, that he might be a merciful and faithful high priest in things pertaining to God, to make reconciliation for the sins of the people. For in that he himself hath suffered being tempted, he is able to succour [help] them that are tempted" (Heb. 2:14-18).

Because of Christ's identity with us we read: "Seeing then that we have a great high priest, that is passed into the heavens, Jesus the Son of God, let us hold fast our profession. For we have not an high priest which cannot be touched with the feeling of our infirmities; but was in all points tempted like as we are, yet without sin. Let us therefore come boldly unto the throne of grace, that we may obtain mercy, and find grace to help in time of need" (4:14-16).

Son of Man and Son of God; human and divine! We do not have trouble with His humanity; that is easy for us to accept. And if we accept the Scriptures, we will have no trouble with His deity. If we do not have a divine Saviour, we have no Saviour at all!

God spoke through the Prophet Isaiah concerning creation: "For thus saith the Lord that created the heavens; God himself that formed the earth and made it; he hath established it, he created it

24

not in vain, he formed it to be inhabited: I am the Lord [Jehovah]; and there is none else" (Isa. 45:18). John did not hesitate to say, "In the beginning was the Word, and the Word was with God, and the Word was God. The same was in the beginning with God. All things were made by him; and without him was not any thing made that was made. . . . And the Word was made flesh, and dwelt among us" (John 1:1-3,14).

Paul wrote: "Giving thanks unto the Father, . . . who hath delivered us from the power of darkness, and hath translated us into the kingdom of his dear Son: in whom we have redemption through his blood, even the forgiveness of sins: who is the image of the invisible God, the firstborn of every creature: for by him were all things created, that are in heaven, and that are in earth, visible and invisible, whether they be thrones, or dominions, or principalities, or powers: all things were created by him, and for him: and he is before all things, and by him all things consist [are held together]" (Col. 1:12-17).

God breathed life into man, and "man became a living soul" (Gen. 2:7). John said of Jesus Christ, "In him was life" (John 1:4), and Jesus said, "I am come that they might have life, and that they might have it more abundantly" (10:10).

The Lord spoke of His saving power through Isaiah: "Before me there was no God formed, neither shall there be after me. I, even I, am the Lord; and beside me there is no saviour" (43:10,11). Yet the angel said to Joseph, "Call his name Jesus: for he shall save his people from their sins" (Matt. 1:21). When He was born in Bethlehem, the angels said to the shepherds, "For

25

unto you is born this day in the city of David a Saviour, which is Christ the Lord" (Luke 2:11). And Jesus announced without reservation that He had come "to seek and to save that which was lost" (19:10).

In Isaiah 44:24 the Lord (Jehovah) calls Himself the Redeemer, yet Paul said of Jesus Christ, "In whom we have redemption through his blood, the forgiveness of sins" (Eph. 1:7). Here is a life we have to reckon with. We ignore Him to our own peril! Our danger comes because we do not conceive of Jesus Christ as being who He really is. If we miss Him, we miss all God has promised and provided concerning our redemption, salvation, justification and eternal life.

Jesus Christ lived as no other; He lived as only God can live. He asked, "Which of you convinceth [convicts] me of sin?" (John 8:46). If we feel overly righteous, all we have to do is try this on for size. If we were to ask, "Who can convict me of any sin?" a thousand voices would reply, "I can!"

Christ died as only God can die. Listen to His words to the dying thief: "To day shalt thou be with me in paradise" (Luke 23:43). No groan of hopelessness but a glad triumph: I will break these shackles, and I will take you with me! Regarding His death He said, "Therefore doth my Father love me, because I lay down my life, that I might take it again. No man taketh it from me, but I lay it down of myself. I have power to lay it down, and I have power to take it again" (John 10:17,18). All men die, but He died as no other; He died for all (II Cor. 5:17-21).

"For the love of Christ constraineth us; because we thus judge, that if one died for all, then

were all dead: and that he died for all, that they which live should not henceforth live unto themselves, but unto him which died for them, and rose again. . . . If any man be in Christ, he is a new creature: old things are passed away; behold, all things are become new. And all things are of God, who hath reconciled us to himself by Jesus Christ, and hath given to us the ministry of reconciliation; to wit [that is], that God was in Christ, reconciling the world unto himself, not imputing their trespasses unto them; and hath committed unto us the word of reconciliation. Now then we are ambassadors for Christ, as though God did beseech you by us: we pray you in Christ's stead, be ye reconciled to God. For he hath made him to be sin for us, who knew no sin; that we might be made the righteousness of God in him" (vv. 14,15,17-21).

He lives now as only God and the redeemed can live—eternally! He rose from the dead and is alive forevermore. The Apostle John saw Him alive: "And when I saw him, I fell at his feet as dead. And he laid his right hand upon me, saying unto me, Fear not; I am the first and the last: I am he that liveth, and was dead; and, behold, I am alive for evermore, Amen; and have the keys of hell and of death" (Rev. 1:17,18).

Christ is the only Saviour and the only Mediator: "For there is one God, and one mediator between God and men, the man Christ Jesus; who gave himself a ransom for all" (I Tim. 2:5,6). He is the only Intercessor: "And they truly were many priests, because they were not suffered to continue by reason of death: but this man, because he continueth ever, hath an unchangeable priesthood. Wherefore he is able also to save them to the uttermost that come unto God by him, seeing he ever liveth to make intercession for them" (Heb. 7:23-25).

He is the one judge who could bring life to the dead, sinful race and present it alive and righteous to God the Father! The great danger is that we will miss the Son! This is so serious that our whole eternal welfare hinges on it! Scripture is as clear as crystal on this: "He that believeth on the Son of God hath the witness in himself: he that believeth not God hath made him a liar; because he believeth not the record that God gave of his Son. And this is the record, that God hath given to us eternal life, and this life is in his Son. He that hath the Son hath life; and he that hath not the Son of God hath not life" (I John 5:10-12).

No wonder the Devil has fought to warp and twist our concept of Jesus Christ. As long as we make Him anything but what He is, we are doomed, and the Devil knows it! He does not care what sweet things we believe about Jesus just as long as we do not believe He is the Son of God and receive Him as personal Saviour! It is strange how we miss this when it is so simple. "God so loved the world, that he gave his only begotten Son, that whosoever believeth in him should not perish, but have everlasting life" (John 3:16).

Chapter 4

A Poor Concept of Grace

The average person knows that our world is in danger today. However, the average person thinks our danger comes from things like pollution, over-population and the use of certain kinds of plastic! That such things present a certain danger cannot be denied. But is there not a greater danger? After all, we—all of us—have but a short while to spend on this earth. While we might prefer to die of old age rather than from poisonous gas or starvation, yet the result is the same. Our real danger may be something vastly different. It seems likely that our real danger is in our poor, or warped, concept of God.

Everyone is familiar with the reaction of a line of dominoes standing on end a half inch apart—they stand or fall together. If the first falls, they all fall. The same is true with our concept of God. If that falls, a lot of things fall with it. If we have no true biblical concept of God, it follows that we have a warped view (sense or concept) of sin. So our concepts, like the line of dominoes, fall one after another because the first one fell. We then have a poor concept of Jesus Christ, and a poor concept of grace will usually follow.

The meaning of the word "grace" is so vast that no single word in English can express it. To grasp it at all, we must narrow it down. As we now view grace, we mean "the disposition to grant something freely." In our context it is God's moving toward us freely and purely because He wills to do so. Grace is God's acting for us in ways we do not deserve and in ways we do not merit. It is God's paying something for us, of His own free will, for which we could not pay. It is a divine favor given to us without any corresponding merit.

No one can read Romans 5:15-21 with understanding and remain the same. Any serious realization of grace has to have some effect on a man who understands it. In Romans 5 Paul set forth God's free gift, not at all to be compared in measure to our sins. His grace goes deeper than the fall of man. It is abounding grace—greater than the offense! Romans 5 calls attention to our dead state, the result of sin, and declares that the grace of God reaches as far as the sin.

We read: "(For if by one man's offence death reigned by one; much more they which receive abundance of grace and of the gift of righteousness shall reign in life by one, Jesus Christ.) Therefore as by the offence of one judgment came upon all men to condemnation; even so by the righteousness of one the free gift came upon all men unto justification of life. For as by one man's disobedience many were made sinners, so by the obedience of one shall many be made righteous. Moreover the law entered, that the offence might abound. But where sin abounded, grace did much more abound: that as sin hath reigned unto death, even so might grace reign through righteousness unto eternal life by Jesus Christ our Lord" (vv. 17-21).

The Apostle Peter referred to God as "the God of all grace" (I Pet. 5:10). He is the God who moves toward men with enough grace to cover everything! He has all the grace needed; no situation, no sin, is big enough to smother His grace. It is all-sufficient grace. It is a great, swelling tide of grace so that every sinner may come, assured of grace enough to cover all his sin.

Dare anyone say that a poor concept of grace is not dangerous? We run from God when we should be running to Him; we hide from Him when we should expose ourselves to Him; we cover our sin when we should confess it. We continue in sin, which condemns us all the more, when there is grace to forgive it! Is not the drowning man in danger if he ignores the lifeboat? If we understood grace, we would flock from north, south, east and west to receive it. Our danger is that, even with grace abounding toward us, we have such a poor concept of it that we miss what it is, what it means and what it does.

While grace is abundant and abounding, it is not cheap. Cheap grace is no grace at all. It is a mistake to equate "free" with "cheap." God acts toward us in grace at fearful cost. God cannot just excuse our sin—that in itself is a deadly misconception. God is holy, and if He were to embrace sin, it would destroy His holiness and His justice. God, in redemption, did something for us which we could not do—He removed a debt from us which we could not pay, and He had to pay that debt Himself. Grace is not God's forgetting our sins, it is God's acting toward us in a way whereby

He can forgive our sin. Grace means that something is free to us, but is was not free to God. God paid a high price in order that you and I might be covered, sheltered by grace.

The actions of God's Son were required to make grace operate, for "the law was given by Moses, but grace and truth came by Jesus Christ" (John 1:17). No man will be met with grace who misses the Son. We, receiving grace, may go free, but Jesus could not. "For all have sinned, and come short of the glory of God; being justified freely by his grace through the redemption that is in Christ Jesus: whom God hath set forth to be a propitiation [atoning sacrifice] through faith in his blood, to declare his righteousness for the remission of sins that are past, through the forbearance of God; to declare, I say, at this time his righteousness: that he might be just, and the justifier of him which believeth in Jesus. Where is boasting then? It is excluded" (Rom. 3:23-27).

Grace does not mean that our penalty for sin, our debt of death, is unpaid. It was paid by another, "for ye know the grace of our Lord Jesus Christ, that, though he was rich, yet for your sakes he became poor, that ye through his poverty might be rich" (II Cor. 8:9). This grace alone brings salvation to us. We are justified through grace and grace alone (Titus 2:11; 3:7). Jesus Christ, God's Son, tasted (experienced) death for every man (Heb. 2:9). No, grace is not cheap. It is tragic that generally our concept of grace has fallen so low. It is amazing and wonderful grace!

Our concept of grace, to be anywhere near what it should be, must include a sense of our need. On what grounds, apart from grace, can we

32

reach God? What will we offer to God as our redemption price? What will we plead that we might be reconciled? What will we use as a covering for our sin? There is only one answer—we need grace. If we are ever to know God, to be reconciled to Him, to stand before Him without condemnation, then He must move toward us in grace. He must act toward us in ways we do not deserve or merit.

If we offer God our righteousness, we have His estimate that "we are all as an unclean thing, and all our righteousnesses are as filthy rags; and we all do fade as a leaf; and our iniquities, like the wind, have taken us away" (Isa. 64:6). If we offer Him our good works, we are saying, in effect, that the work He did was not good enough. "For by grace are ye saved through faith; and that not of yourselves: it is the gift of God: not of works, lest any man should boast. For we are his workmanship, created in Christ Jesus unto good works" (Eph. 2:8-10).

We know, as Jeremiah the prophet knew, that "the way of man is not in himself: it is not in man that walketh to direct his steps" (Jer. 10:23). If we were to offer God wealth, we would hear His word: "They that trust in their wealth, and boast themselves in the multitude of their riches; none of them can by any means redeem his brother, nor give to God a ransom for him: . . . that he should still live for ever, and not see corruption. For he seeth that wise men die, likewise the fool and the brutish person perish, and leave their wealth to others" (Ps. 49:6,7,9,10).

What God does for us is not something He owes us, and it is not anything we can do for ourselves. He who thinks he can find his way to God on his own has never come close to understanding grace. To understand grace is to understand our bankrupt condition, our lostness, our absolutely hopeless state. It is to understand that what has been done, what is being done and all that will ever be done is a work of God, moving toward man to do for us in Christ what we could never do for ourselves.

Grace was not given so that we might continue in the condition in which it found us. It was not given just to cover our sins but to cure us of our sin. Grace not only gives us a new life, it provides us with power to walk in the character of that new life. God's grace—real grace—demands a change, but even that change comes by grace through faith. We are not only saved by His death for us, we are saved by His life in us (Rom. 5:10).

Paul asked the question, "Shall we continue in sin, that grace may abound?" (6:1). Some felt that if God had so much grace, why not use it? Why not continue to sin so God could use more and more of His grace? What was Paul's answer? "God forbid. How shall we that are dead to sin, live any longer therein?" (v. 2). To say that we can continue to sin since grace will cover it is to miss the point of grace altogether. That is to cheapen grace, and God's grace is not cheap. Free, yes; cheap, no!

What God did for us by grace in Christ was to bring us to the place where sin should not have dominion over us (v. 14). "Being then made free from sin, ye became the servants of righteousness" (v. 18). Since everything we have from God is through grace, He resists the proud and gives grace to the humble (James 4:6).

Grace makes us submissive to God, His way and His will. Grace provided for us the cross with all its benefits. Grace supplies the way for us to become the sons of God. Grace brings us to that relationship with God where we have the privilege, past our understanding, of calling Him Father. Our standing is changed, but God remains the same. Grace never allows us to take anything from God's holiness, even though we call Him Father. God always remains full of majesty. God is holy and, therefore, cannot tolerate sin; yet He is so full of grace that we can come to Him when we have sinned, assured that His grace will prove sufficient for us. We are confident of His acceptance, His love and His forgiveness.

But grace means that when we have received divine forgiveness, we come out of that experience with the desire never to sin again. We want to grow in grace, not grovel in sin. We want to know more of our Lord and Saviour, Jesus Christ (II Pet. 3:18), not take advantage of the grace He gives.

No man can, at this time, measure the results of grace. They simply are too vast, too far-reaching. When we become partakers of God's grace through Jesus Christ, the results are seen on earth and in heaven, and they stagger the imagination. Who can measure the depth of grace by which we are translated from the kingdom of darkness into the kingdom of God's dear Son? (Col. 1:13). Who can fathom the grace of God whereby "God, who is rich in mercy, for his great love wherewith he loved us, even when we were dead in sins, hath quickened us [made us alive] together with Christ, (by grace ye are saved;) and hath raised us up together, and made us sit together in heavenly places in Christ Jesus: that in the ages to come he might shew the exceeding riches of his grace in his kindness toward us through Christ Jesus" (Eph. 2:4-7).

Perhaps Paul said it best when he wrote: "Now our Lord Jesus Christ himself, and God, even our Father, which hath loved us, and hath given us everlasting consolation and good hope through grace, comfort your hearts, and stablish you in every good word and work" (II Thess. 2:16,17).

The point of this chapter was to show the danger of a poor concept of grace. Can any man even begin to count the unspeakable loss of missing all that God has provided for us by grace? Can we estimate the danger if we should miss the grace of God since He went to such pains to provide it for us?

Chapter 5

A Poor Concept of the Holy Spirit

Certainly one danger we all face is that which comes from our poor concept of the Holy Spirit. The sinner remains wicked and the saint remains weak because they do not understand the Person and the work of the Holy Spirit. Do we know who He is, where He came from or why He is here? One cannot count up the bad feelings, the heartaches and the broken fellowships resulting from our poor understanding of the Holy Spirit. Certainly this is not His fault but ours. The Devil knows if he can keep us from the work of the Holy Spirit, he has certainly won a battle.

The minute you say "God" you have a mystery. We simply cannot fully understand God. If we could understand all there is to know about our world, every scientific fact, every twist and turn from every point of view, we still would know hardly anything in comparison to what there is to be known. God warns us that His thoughts and ways are not our thoughts and ways: "For as the heavens are higher than the earth, so are my ways higher than your ways, and my thoughts than your thoughts" (Isa. 55:9).

God has chosen to reveal Himself in three

persons—Father, Son and Holy Spirit. All three are God, and God is all three. We do not understand this, but we do not have to understand it. To grasp some of the purpose of God for this age, we can look at things very simply and, while not understanding all there is to know about God, we can learn what He is doing in the world as far as we are concerned. God made our world—the Father, the Son and the Holy Spirit all having a part, for each is mentioned in connection with creation.

God made a man and placed him on the earth which He had made. God told the man what he could do and what he could not do. The man chose not to listen to God. The man lost his right to life as well as his standing before a holy God. God the Son came into the world as a Redeemer; He came to pay the debt of death for the man. While the Son was here fulfilling His part in redemption, and just before He went back to the Father, He said, "And, behold, I send the promise of my Father upon you: but tarry ye in the city of Jerusalem, until ye be endued with power from on high" (Luke 24:49). The Son went back to the Father to mediate for us (I Tim. 2:5) and to intercede for us (Heb. 7:25). Acts 2 contains the record of the coming of the Holy Spirit as the Father had promised the Son. The Holy Spirit is a person, a divine person, and He does what only God can do.

To know something of the Holy Spirit, we can examine His titles. We must realize that names given to diety in scripture designate character. We do not refer to Him as "the Holy Spirit" simply because that happens to be His name. That name tells us what He is like. His name defines His character, His nature. If our concept of the Holy

Spirit is correct, we will remember in our references to Him and in His work in us that He is holy. The Holy Spirit never causes a person to do anything that is unholy. All His work is always in accord with His holy character.

For reasons unknown to me, many people have done terrible things, saying, "God told me to do it." Men have left their wives and families, mistreated their children and a thousand other evil things, giving the excuse that the Spirit of God told them to do it. Of course the Holy Spirit did not tell them to do these things. His very name denies it. The Lord may get the blame from people who do not understand; however, anyone who understands the Holy Spirit knows at once that someone is all mixed up, and it is not the Holy Spirit!

The Holy Spirit is called the "Spirit of grace" (Heb. 10:29). He is here on earth, administering the grace of God, making it real, applying it to the hearts of those who will receive it. Anything the Holy Spirit does will be full of grace. He is holy and gracious. The lack of graciousness in the world, and even in the church, is not the fault of the Holy Spirit. The lack comes from our poor concept of what the Holy Spirit is really like. It was said of the Lord Jesus, "And all ... wondered at the gracious words which proceeded out of his mouth" (Luke 4:22).

The Holy Spirit delights to make us speak gracious words too. Scripture admonishes us, "Let no corrupt communication proceed out of your mouth, but that which is good to the use of edifying, that it may minister grace unto the hearers" (Eph. 4:29), and "Let your speech be alway with grace" (Col. 4:6). What words would be unsaid, what wounds would be healed if we could get the gracious Person of the Holy Spirit into our everyday living!

The Holy Spirit is also called the "Spirit of his Son" (Gal. 4:6). The Holy Spirit will never act in a way that is contrary to the will, the word or the work of the Son. As the Son was holy, so is the Spirit holy. As the Father does and as the Son did, so does the Spirit. Jesus said of the Spirit, "When he, the Spirit of truth, is come, he will guide you into all truth: for he shall not speak of himself; but whatsoever he shall hear, that shall he speak: and he will shew you things to come. He shall glorify me: for he shall receive of mine, and shall shew it unto you. All things that the Father hath are mine: therefore said I, that he shall take of mine, and shall shew it unto you" (John 16:13-15).

The Holy Spirit is also named "Spirit of the living God" (II Cor. 3:3) and "Spirit of the Lord" (Acts 8:39). While we think of God as being distinctly three persons, the Father, Son and Holy Spirit always work together, always in perfect harmony, in perfect oneness. As one is, so is the other.

The Holy Spirit is also called the "Spirit of truth" (John 14:17). He loves the truth. He came to reveal to the ages the truth of Jesus Christ through the Word. He always speaks the truth. He will not flatter us when we need some word of conviction. He will not fail us when we need some word of encouragement—if we are in a position to receive it. There is a lot of false comfort. How can you comfort a man that has no hope? The Holy Spirit will not comfort us in our sin—men may, but He will not. He will convict us of sin and lead us, if we will be led, to a place where we can receive forgiveness and then encouragement. If you want the truth about yourself, listen to the Holy Spirit as He applies the Word of God to your case.

Thus, the Holy Spirit is holy, divine, gracious and truthful. Can we not see the danger of living without Him?

We cannot speak now of all the Holy Spirit does—that would fill volumes. Perhaps we can mention a few things which will help us understand Him better. When you remember that the Holy Spirit is administering the will and the work of the Father and the Son, you can see how great a part He should have in every life.

The Holy Spirit, through the work of the Son, gives access to the Father (Eph. 2:18). He strengthens us with power in the inner man (3:16); He sanctifies (Rom. 15:16; II Thess. 2:13); He baptizes the believer into the Body of Christ (I Cor. 12:13); He convicts (John 16:8); He teaches (Luke 12:12); He comforts (John 14:26); He regenerates (Titus 3:5); He speaks (Acts 11:12; I Tim. 4:1); He helps us in prayer, "for we know not what we should pray for as we ought" (Rom. 8:26); He leads (v. 14); He invites people to the Saviour (Rev. 22:17); He gives life (John 3:5); He adopts into the family of God (Rom. 8:15); He bears witness to salvation (v. 16); and He gives gifts to men for our profit (I Cor. 12:7). For us to miss the work of the Holy Spirit is to miss all. It is to live without help or hope.

Years ago I discovered that God by His Spirit always reveals Himself to us according to our need. The Holy Spirit does not come, for instance, to comfort me in my rebellious and sinful state. This could never be! Being the Spirit of holiness and truth, He goes right to the heart of the matter and convicts me of my sin. That is where the need exists. Jesus said, "When he is come, he will reprove [convict] the world of sin, and of righteousness, and of judgment: of sin, because they believe not on me; of righteousness, because I go to my Father, and ye see me no more; of judgment, because the prince of this world is judged" (John 16:8-11). If I will yield to His conviction concerning my sin, then He can lead me to the Saviour, where I find the needs of my heart met. But He cannot lead me and feed me if I continue in my sin and rebellion. God starts with us in conviction. He strikes at the root of the matter.

We do not have to yield to the Holy Spirit. Thousands are walking this earth this minute who know something of His conviction but have not yielded to Him. The Holy Spirit can be quenched—kept from working (I Thess. 5:19); He can be resisted—His action withstood or fended off (Acts 7:51); and He can be grieved—made to feel sorrow and distress at our hardness of heart (Eph. 4:30). We can become proficient in our rejection of the Holy Spirit; the Bible calls it having our "conscience seared" (I Tim. 4:2).

The Holy Spirit starts with conviction because nothing more can be done for us until we admit our need. Conviction causes us to say, "I am wrong; I did it; I am guilty." When we yield to the conviction of the Holy Spirit by admitting our need, He graciously puts a hunger in our hearts—a hunger for change, a hunger expressed, "I do not want to be this way." When we admit our need and allow the Holy Spirit to give us a hunger to change,

He then intensifies the hunger into a deep desire, a desire that says not only, "I want to be different," but also, "I must, I will, be different." Then the Holy Spirit gives us faith to receive the Saviour, who forgives us and changes us from the inside out.

Such a work cannot be measured in terms of time; from conviction to faith in Christ may be a long or a short period of time. But if it is a real work, the Spirit will always start with conviction and end with faith in the Saviour—a faith that receives Him as personal Lord.

When we receive the Saviour, the Lord Jesus Christ, the Holy Spirit imparts a new life to us (John 6:63; II Cor. 3:6). We receive "great and precious promises: that by these ye might be partakers of the divine nature, having escaped the corruption that is in the world through lust" (II Pet. 1:4). The Holy Spirit is the seal of God on that person and is the sign of a finished transaction and the proof of ownership (Eph. 1:13,14). The believer has been taken out of the old kingdom of darkness and translated into the kingdom of God's dear Son (Col. 1:13).

When a man is convicted of sin and confesses Christ as Lord and Saviour, a sign goes up over that life—Under New Management. The Holy Spirit comes to live in that person, to indwell him. I cannot tell you how this happens, I only know it is true. Neither do I know how my human spirit was captured in my body and lives there. I do not know what keeps it there; I do know it stays only as long as I live. I do not know why it does not escape when I sneeze or slip away some night when I am asleep and cannot watch it. I do not even know how it will leave when death comes upon me. I know I live, and I accept it as it is. Just so, I need not explain how the Holy Spirit comes to dwell in a person. I just know He does.

The knowledge is not based, however, on feeling; it is based on fact. God's Word is clear as can be in the matter: "However you are not in the flesh but in the Spirit, if indeed the Spirit of God dwells in you" (Rom. 8:9, NASB); "Know ye not that ye are the temple of God, and that the Spirit of God dwelleth in you?" (I Cor. 3:16); "What? Know ye not that your body is the temple of the Holy Ghost which is in you, which ye have of God, and ye are not your own? For ye are bought with a price: therefore glorify God in your body, and in your spirit, which are God's" (6:19,20). The Holy Spirit is in us to conform us, as rapidly as He can, to the image of God's dear Son—to live like Jesus Christ (see Eph. 1:11,12; Rom. 8:29).

A poor concept of the Holy Spirit has caused a lot of grief, even among the true children of God. Some have not been taught concerning what the Holy Spirit will do for them. They have heard all sorts of tales about how the Holy Spirit will cause one to do all manner of strange and odd things, and they are afraid. What He does may seem strange to some, and for that I am profoundly thankful. Did not Peter say that some would think us strange and speak evil of us when we did not run with them in rioting? (see I Pet. 4:4). We must realize that no matter what we do, someone is not going to like it. Therefore, we might just as well live for God and let the chips fall where they may.

But do not forget that the Holy Spirit is holy. He is not necessarily interested that you act like everybody else; He is interested that you act like

God—in a righteous manner. Who knows best concerning our lives, we or God? The Holy Spirit seeks to control our lives, not to stifle, hinder or hurt us. He seeks to save the total life and its total ministry and influence.

The command, then, is "Be not drunk with wine, wherein is excess," which is to say, Do not be controlled by that old system of living, do not be pushed into the mold made by the world about you (see Rom. 12:2), "but be filled with [controlled by] the Spirit" (Eph. 5:18). It is one thing to have the Holy Spirit in you and another to have Him in total control of your life. This control does not happen by accident. It is a work of faith, which means that somewhere, sometime, you get off the throne of your life and, with a will and on purpose, give that throne to Him.

If our concept of the Holy Spirit were what it ought to be, we would never even think of trying to run our own lives—experience has told us a thousand times what failures we are at it! It is ridiculous to think we can manage them as well as He can. Almost all our troubles come from our failure to yield the total control of our lives to Him. He should be in charge of everything that comes into the life or goes out of the life. When we run our lives, all sorts of fleshly things creep in and creep out: gossip, ill feelings, touchiness, an unforgiving spirit, jealousy and many more. What grief we have suffered because we continue to manage our own lives. The Holy Spirit is willing, ready and able to manage them for us and to do it as it should be done.

People often say that the Lord, His Word and, sometimes, His people are not practical. And sometimes His people do have ideas of piety that are not practical. But if the Word of God is not practical, if it does not move right into our life situation, then I know of nothing that does.

If you have been listening, you have been hearing a lot of talk about love. Everybody says the world needs love. We have cute, clever signs assuring us that we should smile since God loves us! It is the constant chatter from the high and the low, the rich and the poor—we need more love. Races are accused of not loving other races, and it is said that love would solve, or at least help solve, the differences. Nations are accused of not loving one another, and of course they do not. Can races love or hate? Races and nations are impersonal—they neither love nor hate. People love and people hate. All are agreed that more love, much love, is needed.

And what talk of peace! If we only had peace in our nations, our cities, our homes and our hearts! It would be grand if we did not need a justice of the peace to keep peace. And there is the great need for compassion—for people to care about people, to accept each other, to help, encourage and lift one another.

James Whitcomb Riley said this well in his poem "In a Friendly Sort O' Way":

When a man ain't got a cent, and he's feeling kind o' blue,
An' the clouds hang dark an' heavy, an' won't let the
    sunshine through,
It's a great thing, O my brethren, for a feller just to lay
His hand upon your shoulder in a friendly sort o' way!

It makes a man feel curious, it makes the teardrops start,
An' you sort o' feel a flutter in the region of the heart:

You can look up and meet his eyes; you don't know what
  to say
When his hand is on your shoulder in a friendly sort o' way.

Oh, the world's a curious compound, with its honey and its
  gall,
With its cares and bitter crosses, but a good world, after all.
An' a good God must have made it—leastways, that is what
  I say,
When a hand is on my shoulder in a friendly sort o' way.

And we need more gentleness. We are prone to
go our roughshod way over a lot of others, no
matter who gets hurt. And goodness—we surely
could use a lot of that—just old-fashioned goodness. Combine that with a good dose of meekness,
which is not weakness but a soothing disposition.
That would strip us of some of our snobbish pride,
and things would be a lot better everywhere. And
self-control! People are too rebellious. They lose
their tempers over nothing and act like spoiled
babies. We could use a considerable amount of
self-control.

That is practical talk, we say. That is getting
down to earth where the real need is. Indeed it is,
but do we know that we are talking of nothing
more or less than the "fruit of the Spirit"? (Gal.
5:22). These are the very things the Holy Spirit
begins to bring forth in the life over which He has
control. Let no man talk of things that are reason-
able or needed or practical in this world until he
has considered the fruit of the Spirit. The desire of
the Holy Spirit is that people behave as they
should. He wants them to live in love, in peace, in
joy, with a concern for others, in gentleness, goodness and meekness, with self-control and with faith

47

in God, here and now—today—right where we live at the moment.

What loss we have suffered, what heartaches we have endured, what hate has eaten away at us, what bitterness we have tasted, what selfishness we have shown, all because we have a poor concept of the Holy Spirit. We know far too little of who He is and what He does. The danger is that we will continue to go our own way and miss so very much in this life—and even more in the life to come.

Chapter 6

A Poor Concept of Time

It is altogether possible that many people do not consider the claims of the gospel because they have a poor concept of time. In fact, many things might get straightened out in a hurry if we realized that time might catch us with the really important things undone.

The following story illustrates this point. Two men held hard feelings toward each other for many years. One was on his sickbed and was not expected to live. He called the other man into his room and got everything straightened out. Just as the well man was about to leave, the sick one said, "Now if I live, the deal is off. I just wanted everything to be right if I should die!" We laugh at such foolishness, but laughter is often nothing more than an admission of our own guilt.

What we know about time and what we do about it are often not the same. Every experience tells us time is short. We all see the older generation passing steadily and surely on. We know it will be our turn soon; yet, somehow we always think it will happen years from now, somewhere in the foggy future.

I remember speaking to a dying man who was 70 years old. He agreed that men ought to be prepared for death. When pressed to make some definite commitment to the Lord, his reply was, "Not now, I've been sick many times before; I've always come out of it, and therefore I will this time too." He just could not think that time had run out for him.

God is timeless; we are creatures of time. God made time for us. When God prepared the world for man, He moved the stars, the moon and the sun into time arrangements for us. He appointed them "for seasons, and for days, and years" (Gen. 1:14). God did not need them as measurements of time for Himself; He knew what time it was without reference to anything. There is no past or future with God. Everything that has ever happened with God is as though it were happening now.

Thus, judgment is no problem with God. We do not understand how God can judge all the past acts of men. We surmise that since we forget them, God will forget them. It seems quite easy for us to think that God might judge the wrongs of today if the judgment were today, but we somehow feel that God will, as we do, forget the wrongs with the passing of time. But God does not forget. Every wicked act of every man must one day march before God and be judged. We cannot understand how it will be done, but with God time is not a problem. The only thing God remembers no more are the sins that are confessed and forgiven on the basis of faith in the redeeming work of God's Son, Jesus Christ (Jer. 31:34; I John 1:9).

With God everything that will ever happen is as though it were happening now. Therefore, He can predict the future as well as remember the past. God spoke to Jeremiah, saying, "Before I formed thee in the belly I knew thee; and before thou camest forth out of the womb I sanctified thee" (Jer. 1:5). God spoke through His prophets, giving details of things which were to happen centuries later. Prophecy is nothing but history before it happens. God is not hedged in by time—past or future. God is not pressed for time. "One day is with the Lord as a thousand years, and a thousand years as one day" (II Pet. 3:8), which is to say that time really does not matter to God at all. But time is a very important part of our lives. We have an allotted time for life and do not know how long it is. Some have very little. We all know that our time could be up tomorrow, but we act as though it just could not be!

It would seem that if God went out of His way to impress us with anything in the Scriptures, it was the shortness of our allotted lifetime. A thread which runs through the Scriptures keeps calling out to us, "Hurry, hurry, hurry!" Once Paul was writing concerning getting married. Times were hard; there were some other factors involved, and Paul was giving advice on the matter. The question was, All things being equal, should a man get married or not? In all of this Paul reminded them of one thing: "The time is short; . . . for the fashion of this world passeth away" (I Cor. 7:29,31).

David, considering the length of his life, said, "Thou hast made my days as an handbreadth" (Ps. 39:5). The hand was used as an instrument of measurement in those days. Now, if this measure is used at all, it means about four inches, or the width of the back of a man's hand. (About the only use it has today, to my knowledge, is in determining the height of horses; they are declared to be so many hands high.) David could have held up his hand, his four-inch—wide hand, and compared it to that measureless space. Four inches against all the distance in the universe! Our lives are like that.

King Hezekiah lamented that his age was departed and removed "as a shepherd's tent: I have cut off like a weaver my life" (Isa. 38:12). Shepherds had to live in such a way that they could move at a moment's notice. Many reasons combined to make this necessary. They were here today and gone tomorrow. Hezekiah saw life like that—here today and gone tomorrow. He said life was like a weaving. As the weaver finished the piece on which he was working and cut the thread, so was life. We do not know when the pattern for us will be finished and the thread cut—that tiny, flimsy thread!

We are all familiar with the comparison of life to flowers and grass. Pastors often use this figure of speech at the graveside. The Bible says, "As for man, his days are as grass: as a flower of the field, so he flourisheth. For the wind passeth over it, and it is gone; and the place thereof shall know it no more" (Ps. 103:15,16). Such a thing has to be seen to be believed. Pharaoh and Joseph evidently knew. Pharaoh dreamed of ears of grain "blasted with the east wind" (Gen. 41:6), and Joseph said they stood for seven years of famine. Those of us who have lived in dry areas of the world and have seen fresh, green crops curl and die in two or three days can easily understand the uncertainty of life referred to by the wind's passing over the grass and flower.

Job looked at his days as "swifter than a post: they flee away, they see no good. They are passed away as the swift ships: as the eagle that hasteth to the prey" (Job 9:25,26). The "post" was a swift runner carrying royal letters and dispatches throughout the kingdom (see II Chron. 30:6). In Persia they were mounted on swift horses. Almost everyone remembers the story of Queen Esther. When the plot to destroy her people had been discovered, a hurried message had to go to the ends of the kingdom. Mordecai, Esther's uncle, wrote the message in the name of the king, sealed it with the king's ring and "sent letters by posts on horseback, and riders on mules, camels, and young dromedaries [swift camels]" (Esther 8:10).

In the early 1860s the western United States had what was known as the "pony express"—a system of carrying and delivering mail by riders on horses that could travel far and fast. They changed horses along the way so as to move as rapidly as possible. Some of the riders made incredible time.

In reference to Job, we must remember that the swiftest thing he knew on land was a post, or a swift messenger. We often forget that until just a comparatively few years ago, we could travel no faster than people could in Job's time.

The fastest thing Job had ever seen on water was some type of sailboat. So he likened life to the swift ships that passed by. He perhaps had seen them as they appeared on the horizon in the evening, and the next morning they had disappeared on the other horizon. Life, said Job, is like that.

Then he caught sight of the eagle in its plummet to snatch its prey. Ah, said Job, life is like that! It is as a post, a swift ship and an eagle hastening to the prey—the swiftest thing on land, on sea and in the air. Nothing could point up his message more clearly; he was measuring life by the swiftest things he knew. See the post run! See the ships sail with the wind! See the eagle hastening to the prey! Remember, life is like that.

In chapter 7 Job used another illustration to remind us of life's uncertainty. "Is there not an appointed time to man upon earth? Are not his days also like the days of an hireling?" (v. 1). Life, said Job, is like someone working for an employer who can bring his work to a close at any time he so desires. Man does not know the day his labor is over.

Scripture likens life to smoke (Ps. 102:3) and vapor (James 4:14). You cannot take hold of smoke or vapor. They are there and then they are gone. Every thinking person would agree with David: "Mine age is as nothing before thee" (Ps. 39:5).

> Tomorrow you will live, you always cry;
> In what far country does this morrow lie,
> That 'tis so mighty long ere it arrive?
> Beyond the Indies does this morrow live?
> 'Tis so far fetched, this morrow, that I fear
> 'Twill be both very old and very dear.
> Tomorrow I will live, the fool does say;
> To-day itself's too late: the wise lived yesterday.
> —Marcus Valerius Martialis
> (tr. Abraham Cowley)

The fact of the shortness of time has escaped many of us. We live as though we would live forever. Our concept of time is twisted, warped, out of focus. We procrastinate, forgetting that we are about to run out of time. The tomorrows will not always keep tumbling down on our heads.

The Bible generally urges us to calmness, to quietness, to peace and to rest. God moves and wants us to move with a certain, calm assurance. "I lay in Zion for a foundation a stone, a tried stone, a precious corner stone, a sure foundation: he that believeth shall not make haste" (Isa. 28:16).

The exception to this is when the matter of our salvation is at stake. On that point the Scriptures know nothing but urgency. In II Corinthians 6:2 Paul quoted from Isaiah the prophet: "For he saith, I have heard thee in a time accepted, and in the day of salvation have I succoured thee: behold, now is the accepted time; behold, now is the day of salvation." No margin for dillydallying there.

"Wherefore (as the Holy Ghost saith, To day if ye will hear his voice, harden not your hearts, as in the provocation, in the day of temptation in the wilderness)" (Heb. 3:7,8). "Again, he limiteth a certain day, saying in David, To day, after so long a time; as it is said, To day if ye will hear his voice, harden not your hearts" (4:7).

There is no more pointed word than that of James 4:13-17: "Come now, you who say, 'Today or tomorrow, we shall go to such and such a city, and spend a year there and engage in business and make a profit.' Yet you do not know what your life will be like tomorrow. You are just a vapor that appears for a little while and then vanishes away. Instead, you ought to say, 'If the Lord wills, we shall live and also do this or that.' But as it is, you boast in your arrogance; all such boasting is

55

evil. Therefore, to one who knows the right thing to do, and does not do it, to him it is sin" (NASB).

Luke 12 illustrates this point quite well: "And he [Jesus] spake a parable unto them, saying, The ground of a certain rich man brought forth plentifully: and he thought within himself, saying, What shall I do, because I have no room where to bestow my fruits? And he said, This will I do: I will pull down my barns, and build greater; and there will I bestow all my fruits and my goods. And I will say to my soul, Soul, thou hast much goods laid up for many years; take thine ease, eat, drink, and be merry. But God said unto him, Thou fool, this night thy soul shall be required of thee: then whose shall those things be, which thou hast provided? So is he that layeth up treasure for himself, and is not rich toward God" (vv. 16-21).

Walt Huntley, a friend of mine, said it well in his poem "Have You Thought About Your Soul?":

> Have you ever stopped to wonder
>   What this life is all about?
> Why you're here and where you're going
>   When your lease on time runs out?
> Maybe you've been far too busy,
>   Trying hard to reach your goal.
> Would you let me ask you kindly,
>   Have you thought about your soul?
>
> You may reach the highest portals,
>   And your dreams may all come true;
> Wealth and fame may be your portion,
>   And success may shine on you.
> All your friends may sing your praises,
>   Not a care on you may roll.
> What about the great tomorrow—
>   Have you thought about your soul?

Don't forget your days are numbered,
    Though you may be ridin' high;
But like all of us poor mortals,
    Someday you'll just up and die.
Your success and fame and glory
    Won't be worth the bell they toll.
Let me ask you just one question:
    Have you thought about your soul?

If you've never thought it over,
    Spend a little time today;
There is nothin' more important
    That will ever come your way
Than the joy of sins forgiven,
    And to know you've been made whole.
In the name of Christ the Saviour,
    Have you thought about your soul?
                            —Walt Huntley

Chapter 7

A Poor Concept of
Our Own Heart

One of the strange things about us is that we know so little about ourselves. You would think that after living in a body for years, we would know all about it, but we certainly do not. For instance, the heart has been there, beating away every minute, night and day, yet we know very little about it. No doubt we have all read about the heart, since much has been written about it. A lot has also been written about the hardening of the arteries. I wonder that so little is written about the hardening of the heart!

Of course, the heart I speak of is not that hollow muscular organ in the chest with right and left auricle and right and left ventricle. The heart I speak of is the center, or source, of emotion, of our personality attributes, where we have our innermost thoughts and feelings. We speak of it when we say we hate or we love "with all our hearts" or "I know it in my heart" or "My heart tells me so." How little we know of that heart!

One thing concerning that heart you never hear about is that, left to itself, it never grows softer with the passing years. The influences of the Holy Spirit make the heart soft and yielding, but apart from that, it can become dangerously hard. Have you ever wondered why it is so much easier to approach a child with spiritual things than most adults? And how easily a child repents or forgives or forgets? Have you ever wondered why Jesus said, "Except ye be converted, and become as little children, ye shall not enter into the kingdom of heaven"? (Matt. 18:3).

Pharaoh's heart did not become softer with age and experience. God, through Moses, rained blow after blow upon Pharaoh to soften his heart so that he would let Israel go, but he continually hardened his heart.

When the Israelites were delivered from the bondage of slavery, their hearts did not grow softer. They showed such disobedience and hardness of heart and rebellion that God had to judge them for it. This is recorded for us as a lesson, a warning: "Harden not your heart, as in the provocation, and as in the day of temptation in the wilderness: when your fathers tempted me, proved me, and saw my work. Forty years long was I grieved with this generation, and said, It is a people that do err in their heart, and they have not known my ways: unto whom I sware in my wrath that they should not enter into my rest" (Ps. 95:8-11).

The warning continues: "For he established a testimony in Jacob, and appointed a law in Israel, which he commanded our fathers, that they should make them known to their children: that the generation to come might know them, even the children which should be born; who should arise and declare them to their children: that they might

60

set their hope in God, and not forget the works of God, but keep his commandments: and might not be as their fathers, a stubborn and rebellious generation; a generation that set not their heart aright, and whose spirit was not stedfast with God" (Ps. 78:5-8).

We simply do not understand that our hearts do not naturally grow soft with the passing of time. It is dangerous to have a mistaken concept of one's own heart. To think that making right decisions concerning God and grace will be easier tomorrow is to admit we understand nothing about our hearts. I wonder that we have not given more thought to this when we are surrounded with so much evidence.

We are a generation that screams reality, yet we hardly ever face it. We often picture older people as the sweet little old grandmother and the gentle old grandfather. It does happen, but that picture is the exception and not the rule. True, Grandpa is more gentle on the outside; he has to be, not because his heart is soft but because his muscles are. But touch him where he really lives, listen to him, watch him and see what he is really like. Does he have a gentle spirit? Does he have a pure mind? Is he agreeable and kind? Are all the relatives clamoring to have him around? Is he considerate and compassionate? If we were to be truthful, we would have to say just the opposite is generally true. How many old people are bitter and hard? How many are "nice" old people? Some I have known become suddenly hard and hostile when you mention something concerning the Lord. Why? Life is pretty well gone, time is running out; they will soon be on the other side of the dark river. Surely now their hearts will be soft, but often they are not. Hearts do not grow softer just because we grow older; in all likelihood they will grow harder.

Many people do not respond to the gospel because they do not recognize their danger, and one danger is a poor concept of our own heart. We simply do not understand that, left to themselves, hearts grow harder as the days go by. Many small samplings have been taken to find the age at which people have believed in the Lord. The percentage is high among the younger ones and runs dangerously low in the older years. Does God cease to love us when we grow older? Of course not. The fact is, our hearts just keep getting harder and harder, and they do not readily respond to the gospel. The will weakens, and the heart hardens.

It is no accident that the Bible always emphasizes the importance of receiving salvation now. God knows that time runs out for us all, but we do not know the time. Thus, our eternal decisions are pressing. But even if we do have some time left—even many years—can we be assured that more time will make our decisions for God, good, righteousness and redemption any easier? "Man that is born of a woman," the Bible says, "is of few days, and [they are] full of trouble" (Job 14:1). It could well be that you and I have but few days left. But even if, in the mercies of God, several years were left in our allotted time, are we sure the passing of time will soften us toward God or toward sin? "Now is the day of salvation" (II Cor. 6:2) are not idle words. "To day if ye will hear his voice, harden not your heart" (Ps. 95:7,8) may seem to be a sentimental plea of the Spirit, but it is also a sensible plea of the Spirit.

What pointed lessons there are here for parents! Parents often say they are not going to make decisions for their children. They will let them grow up and make their own decisions. Why do they suppose the Scriptures say, "Train up a child in the way he should go: and when he is old, he will not depart from it"? (Prov. 22:6). If parents are not responsible enough to make decisions, they are not responsible enough to have children in the first place. Don't we parents know that 90 percent of the time our children follow us not only in social patterns but also in spiritual patterns? The undisciplined child who has had no decisions made for him, who knows nothing of guidance of both body and spirit, has not a ghost of a chance in our world. His heart needs that gentle discipline while he is young, tender and teachable.

Someone said, "Make your educational laws strict and your criminal laws may be gentle; but leave youth its liberty and you will have to dig dungeons for age." To put that in modern-day language is to say, If you do not train and teach and discipline your children in youth, they will throw you out when you are old. It is no laughing matter.

David, that great king, had a son of whom we have a sad record. First we are told, "His father had not displeased him at any time in saying, Why hast thou done so?" (I Kings 1:6). A novice could have predicted the outcome. The son "exalted himself, saying, I will be king" (v. 5). Only a quick move on the part of Nathan the prophet saved the king his kingdom. David did not follow what Jeremiah later wrote: "It is good for a man that he bear the yoke in his youth" (Lam. 3:27).

Solomon was also to write wise words later: "Hear me now therefore, O ye children, and depart not from the words of my mouth.... Lest ... thou mourn at the last, ... and say, How have I hated instruction, and my heart despised reproof; and have not obeyed the voice of my teachers, nor inclined mine ear to them that instructed me!" (Prov. 5:7,10-13). What more can be said to show, caution, warn, admonish, shock and exhort a person to "keep thy heart with all diligence; for out of it are the issues of life"? (4:23).

David said, "As the hart [deer] panteth after the water brooks, so panteth my soul after thee, O God" (Ps. 42:1). Little do any of us realize what God can do with a man whose heart is right toward Him. We sometimes think, in the hardness of our hearts, that God delights in punishing the evildoer. This is about as far from the truth as we can get. God delights in mercy. His call is "Turn you at my reproof: behold, I will pour out my spirit unto you, I will make known my words unto you" (Prov. 1:23).

There seems to be no limit to what God can and will do in a yielded heart. He will strengthen the hearts of those who wait on Him (Ps. 27:14); He will give joy to the upright in heart (32:11); He will save the broken in heart (34:18); He will give the desires of their hearts to those who delight in Him (37:4); He will keep the steps of the man who has God's law in his heart (v. 31); and He will create a clean heart in the repentant (51:10).

For the hard in heart God can do nothing. The bitter in heart can know no peace. The bitter in heart are never happy. They have, in their estimation, been wronged, mistreated or overlooked; but their thoughts are warped by their own bitterness. Every man ought to take immediate, serious inventory of his heart, lest he be as Paul said: "Because of your stubbornness and unrepentant heart you are storing up wrath for yourself in the day of wrath and revelation of the righteous judgment of God" (Rom. 2:5, NASB).

Psalm 139 is the picture of God's searching a man's heart—his deep, inner life. This was David's heart, and it frightened him to know that God knew everything. God knew where he sat down, when he got up, where he walked, what he said and even what he meant by what he said. His first reaction to such knowledge was to want to get as far away from God as possible: "Whither shall I flee from thy presence?" (v. 7). But, he reasoned, if he went to heaven, to hell or even to the "uttermost parts of the sea" (v. 9), God would be there. The darkness does not cover us (startling revelation though that may be to a lot of people), for the darkness and the light are both visible to God.

There is only one way to turn, only one sensible thing to do: Yield to God—stop running from Him and come to Him. This David did. He invited God into the very center of everything and closed the passage with "Search me, O God, and know my heart: try me, and know my thoughts: and see if there be any wicked way in me, and lead me in the way everlasting" (vv. 23,24).

An old saying states, "A man may not be what he thinks he is, but what he thinks, he is." Proverbs 23:7 agrees: "For as he thinketh in his heart, so is he." If we ever get a clear concept of the possibilities both for good and for evil locked in our hearts and at the same time realize that time is always very precious, it will stir us to sober examination and careful action to assure ourselves of a soft heart. The Psalms are right and clear on this point when they say, "Blessed is the man whose strength is in thee; in whose heart are the ways of them" (84:5). Blessed is the man in whose heart are God's ways, in whose heart are the highways of heaven and in whose heart God has an acknowledged right to walk and work.

Chapter 8

A Poor Concept of Judgement

One thing we are clearly unaware of today is the judgments of God. We have been raised on a diet of the goodness of man and the fatherhood of God until we have lost all sense of God's righteousness and a judgment to come. Who speaks faithfully today of reaping what we sow? Any suggestion that we might be doing wrong and must face a judgment is quickly hushed. To speak of right and wrong and conscience and judgment is labeled old-fashioned—and we must not be old-fashioned! Strange thing, though, that we can teach a generation that they are not responsible to any moral code, that sin is a carry-over from the Dark Ages and that judgment was a gimmick of the Middle Ages to keep people in line; but we cannot teach them how to handle guilt, how to have peace or how to find the meaning of life. We have given them stones for bread and serpents for fish (see Matt. 7:9,10).

If a person has a poor concept of judgment, he is not likely to have a very clear concept of his responsibilities in life. Uncounted dangers lie hidden in our poor understanding of the judgment of God. We have treated judgment the way we treat shadows in the dark: Ignore them, look the other way, and they will all go away. We may not realize it, but in our times we are faced with some sober decisions. If we continue to label sin as sickness, weakness or slight mistakes, if we make salvation nothing more than a better understanding of our social responsibilities to one another, if we outlaw the judgments of God on disobedience, we may find we have taken away more than we can afford.

Are we to become a generation which does what is right in its own eyes? (see Prov. 12:15). Or are we to become a generation that is responsible to God's Word? Our view of judgment may make the difference. Time will tell, but we do not have much time left in which to decide. Let us not try to blame the generation that follows our own for all that has gone wrong. Who taught the coming generation that they had no responsibility to parents, to neighbors or to God? Who took away a gospel for sinners and gave in its place a social gospel? Who said that marriage and the home are not important and that morality is an old wives' tale? We certainly cannot pin that on the younger generation.

Great changes undoubtedly would take place from the humble home to the highest offices of the land if we got our view of judgment in focus. Jesus spoke of the "danger of the judgment" (Matt. 5:21). He evidently did not think it was any laughing matter! The Bible speaks of "eternal judgment" (Heb. 6:2)—judgment which has eternal consequences. It might not hurt us, and it may do us a lot of good, to have an honest look at the judgment of God.

About the first thing you would notice about

judgment, if you looked seriously, would be that it is not what most people think it is. Mr. Average Man does not have the foggiest notion concerning judgment; if he did, it would certainly greatly affect his actions.

People sometimes argue that the only judgment we know is on this earth—a sort of balancing act of nature. The argument goes like this: If I steal my neighbor's goods, something, sooner or later, will happen to my goods. This is the reasoning of children.

But anybody who faces life realistically knows there has to be a judgment somewhere in the future when an all-knowing God sets things straight and measures out judgment with all the facts of the case clearly in view. There are judgments in this life; we see them all the time. But that great day of judgment, when all stand before God, comes after death: "And as it is appointed unto men once to die, but after this the judgment" (9:27).

A lot of unsolved devilment dies with some people. History knows of a thousand wrongs that are buried beneath the sod, unknown by any living person. Homes have been broken, lives ruined, children hurt, the poor trampled underfoot, the innocent hanged or murdered; the story is too long and too painful for us to linger on it. What about it? Are we simply to forget all that? We say we live in a new day. We are enlightened, and we are building a better world. We are going to banish war; we are going to heal our sick society so our homes will be safe; we are going to teach people how to behave; we are going to banish poverty from the earth. Excellent! A worthy goal indeed! But what about the past? Do we just ring the curtain down and forget that those who lived in the yesterdays were people too? Is justice only for our enlightened time? Do we write those people of yesterday off as a necessary expenditure in the upward struggle for sanity? And what if we fail to shape the world into the mold of which we dream? You would not get great odds on a bet that our world will break out in a rash of righteousness very soon.

No, if there is to be any reason, any hope for justice at all, then there must be a judgment to come, when all the living and the dead answer for their deeds. Reason does not speak alone—the Bible is clear that no one escapes judgment. It does include all the dead and all the living (see Acts 10:42). Death does not detour judgment. At the time of judgment it matters not if a person is alive, if he has been dead for a thousand years or if he dies one day before the judgment—all come to judgment.

In the judgment we are measured by several things, and these things are seldom what we think are important. First, judgment is measured by quality of life. Do we appear at the judgment alive or dead? No, I am not referring to whether we are living or have died at the judgment but to this: When we appear at the judgment, are we living people or dead people? Life is more than existence. We all know that physical death has passed on all men (Rom. 5:12)—we see it all the time. But what a lot of us do not realize is that we not only die physically, we are dead spiritually—dead in trespasses and sins (Eph. 2:1)—cut off from God. The good news, the gospel, is that Christ died for our sins (I Cor. 15:1-4). He came that we might have life (John 10:10). In Christ we get back that life we lost through sin.

Jesus said, "And this is life eternal, that they might know thee the only true God, and Jesus Christ, whom thou hast sent" (17:3). "And this is the record," said the Apostle John, "that God hath given to us eternal life, and this life is in his Son" (I John 5:11). So the first consideration is, Do we know a Saviour who dealt with our sin and gave us eternal life? Eternal life in Christ determines our destiny. You can begin to understand why our poor concept of judgment is such a danger. Ignorance is never bliss, especially when it relates to judgment.

Another measurement in judgment is our works. Almost everybody has some idea about this aspect of judgment. They see God with a great balance in His hand. At the judgment He takes their good works and places them on one side of the balance; then He places their bad works on the other side of the balance. If the good outweighs the bad, they go skipping off to heaven. If the bad outweighs the good, well, God is good, isn't He? He'll surely work something out, won't He? The great fallacy is in thinking that works determine destiny. No clearer statement can be made on the matter than "By grace are ye saved through faith; and that not of yourselves: it is the gift of God: not of works, lest any man should boast" (Eph. 2:8,9). If even one man could get to heaven on his good works, the death of Jesus Christ would have been in vain. Works only determine the measure of reward for those who have confessed their sin and received new life in Christ the Saviour and to

71

measure the punishment for those who have come to judgment without this new life.

At the judgment nothing will be secret. It staggers us to think of what the judgment will reveal. Imagine evil men who thought they got by with murder and laughed at their cleverness, their power and their wit. Suddenly they are called to judgment and are confronted with every speck of evidence and are judged, not as clever, powerful and wise, but as murderers. There are no "wise guys" at the judgment.

Judgment is according to our words (Matt. 12:36), according to our ungodly deeds (Jude 1:15) and according to every hidden thing (I Cor. 4:5). "Neither is there any creature that is not manifest in his sight: but all things are naked and opened unto the eyes of him with whom we have to do" (Heb. 4:13). When Jesus was teaching his disciples, He warned them against hypocrisy, saying, "Beware. . . . For there is nothing covered, that shall not be revealed; neither hid, that shall not be known. Therefore whatsoever ye have spoken in darkness shall be heard in the light; and that which ye have spoken in the ear in closets shall be proclaimed upon the housetops" (Luke 12:1-3).

A sober view of the judgment would tighten up a lot of lives and a lot of lips. What changes would be made if we could only remember that there are no secret deals! They are secret only for a time. One day they will all come tumbling out, and every detail will be revealed.

In the judgment men are measured against God's righteousness. "Now [God] commandeth all men every where to repent: because he hath

72

appointed a day, in the which he will judge the world in righteousness by that man whom he hath ordained; whereof he hath given assurance unto all men, in that he hath raised him from the dead" (Acts 17:30,31). Let us not be led astray by thinking we can make things legal by writing laws to fit our own desires and that we can escape the righteousness of God. No man, or set of men, has a right to tamper with that which is clearly given in God's Word.

Jesus said, "I am come a light into the world, that whosoever believeth on me should not abide in darkness. And if any man hear my words, and believe not, I judge him not: for I came not to judge the world, but to save the world. He that rejecteth me, and receiveth not my words, hath one that judgeth him: the word that I have spoken, the same shall judge him in the last day. For I have not spoken of myself; but the Father which sent me, he gave me a commandment, what I should say, and what I should speak. And I know that his commandment is life everlasting" (John 12:46-50).

When it comes to judgment, something seems to be missing in us. We seemingly cannot realize that judgment is coming sure and soon. This was also true in the days before the flood. The idea of a judgment on the earth was unthinkable, but it happened. It was so in the days of Sodom and Gomorrah. They lusted and laughed, they killed and cackled. And one day the fire fell. And it is so with us. We think things will continue as they always have. Peter warned us that people would say, "Where is the promise of his coming? For since the fathers fell asleep, all things continue as they were from the beginning of the creation" (II Pet. 3:4).

The Scriptures are so clear about judgment that a child reading through them would see it. Yet we go on as though life will never end. We throw our lives away as though there will never be an accounting day. It was a great day for the Devil when he got us started thinking lightly about judgment.

If we began to think rightly of the judgment to come, we would surely seek a way to escape it. And we would find it. How to escape judgment is the theme of the Scripture. That is what the cross and the resurrection are all about. Nothing is more clearly set forth in the Scriptures than God's working in our behalf so that we will not have to face the judgment unprepared. Consider the following verses: "For God so loved the world, that he gave his only begotten Son, that whosoever believeth in him should not perish, but have everlasting life. For God sent not his Son into the world to condemn the world; but that the world through him might be saved. He that believeth on him is not condemned: but he that believeth not is condemned already, because he hath not believed in the name of the only begotten Son of God" (John 3:16-18).

"Therefore being justified by faith, we have peace with God through our Lord Jesus Christ" (Rom. 5:1). "There is therefore now no condemnation [judgment] to them which are in Christ Jesus, who walk not after the flesh, but after the Spirit" (8:1). "Who [Jesus] was delivered for our offences, and was raised again for our justification" (4:25).

"But now the righteousness of God without the law is manifested, being witnessed by the law and the prophets; even the righteousness of God which is by faith of Jesus Christ unto all and upon all them that believe: for there is no difference" (3:21,22).

Chapter 9

A Poor Concept of Direction

Not only are we unconcerned about our spiritual lives if we do not know our danger, but our unconcern is strengthened if we do not know our direction. Life has often been compared to a journey, beginning at the cradle and ending at the grave. Without thinking about it for one moment, most of us assume there is no choice in the direction that road will take. We assume every life will somehow end up at the gates of pearl.

If you want to find out whether or not we are sensitive to our direction, ask the next ten persons you meet what is the way to heaven. One answer you will surely get is that it really does not matter what you believe, do or think or how you act, for we are all going to the same place even though we are taking different roads. When Rome was at the height of its power, there was a saying: "All roads lead to Rome." We think the same holds true for the eternal home of man. No matter how we live, no matter what way we choose to go, by some miracle or magic we will all manage to end up at the same place.

We do not reason this way at any other time. If you get on a train going the wrong way, you end up at the wrong place. If you get on a plane or a bus going the wrong way, you end up at the wrong destination. If you start on a journey and go in the wrong direction, you will not end up at the expected location even if you have a thousand people assuring you that it does not matter if you are on the wrong road.

What is the truth of the matter? The truth is that you reach the right destination only by taking the right road—and that's true in matters of the Spirit as well. We choose our direction in life, and our first choice is to go our own way. Just because "all the ways of a man are clean in his own eyes" (Prov. 16:2) does not mean they are God's ways. C. S. Lewis observed that heaven is the habitation of those who say to God, "Thy will be done," whereas hell is the habitation of those to whom God says, "Thy will be done."

We cannot go our way and God's way at the same time; we must make a choice. When the Prophet Jeremiah said, "O Lord, I know that the way of man is not in himself: it is not in man that walketh to direct his steps" (Jer. 10:23), he was admitting that we have chosen the wrong way, the wrong road, and that in ourselves we are powerless to change.

In the beginning, when God made man, things were very good (Gen. 1:27,31). The evidence seems to be that they talked together face to face; certainly the communication was direct (see 2:16,17). Adam named the beasts and the birds (vv. 19,20), and he must have told God why he named them as he did. Adam would surely have needed advice on how to keep and dress the garden (v. 15). Their relationship was that of man and

God walking and talking together. They were in accord. They were both going the same way.

One day as God came walking in the cool of the day, a change had taken place. Adam and Eve had hidden from the presence of God (3:8). To make it very simple, they had changed their direction. They no longer had their face toward God's face. Fellowship was broken; they were afraid. Since fear is so much a part of our world, it is interesting to note that the second recorded words of man are "I heard thy voice in the garden, and I was afraid" (v. 10). Man had chosen a new way for himself—his own way. The situation at that moment was this: God had His face toward man, and man had his back toward God. Sin is the transgression of God's law (I John 3:4), and Adam was making laws of his own.

"All unrighteousness is sin" (I John 5:17). God had told Adam what was right regarding the trees of the Garden, and Adam did what he knew was not right. Then, since God was holy, He could do only one thing—He had to turn His back on man. And the situation at that point was God and man back to back, each going in a different direction, each going separate ways. A child could see that there is no way for God and man to meet if they both keep going in the opposite direction.

There was another problem. God had said, "In the day that thou eatest thereof thou shalt surely die" (Gen. 2:17). God cannot make idle threats or promises. But God loved man; He did not want man to go on in his direction, which leads only to death, or eternal separation from Himself. God decided to turn His face back to man, to call after him, to urge him to change his direction. But man is under the sentence of death. Here enters the whole plan for man's redemption, salvation and justification. The plan was for another to take the place of man and to die for him. God would then be just in keeping His word and could also be the justifier of man, since the penalty would be paid. This is what nearly the whole Bible is about. This justification, redemption and salvation was accomplished through the Old Testament sacrifices for sin, pointing to and fulfilled in God's Son, Jesus Christ.

We read: "God was in Christ, reconciling the world unto himself" (II Cor. 5:19); "And you . . . hath he reconciled in the body of his flesh through death, to present you holy and unblameable and unreproveable in his sight" (Col. 1:21,22). Thus, in the death of His Son, God turned His face back to man. The situation for every man now is that our back is toward God and God's face is toward us. Think of it—God is calling after us and we are just going our own way, unheeding, unthinking and unthankful.

Isaiah stated our condition, our direction, perfectly: "All we like sheep have gone astray; we have turned every one to his own way; and the Lord hath laid on him [His servant Son] the iniquity of us all" (Isa. 53:6). Now we can understand why Jesus said, "Except ye be converted, and become as little children, ye shall not enter into the kingdom of heaven" (Matt. 18:3). "Converted" means to change our way, our mind, our direction. When a man is converted, when he turns from his way, then man and God are back together on peaceful terms. They are fully reconciled. They are in fellowship. God has done all He can do; the decision is up to us.

We are not without warning that our direction is very important. Jesus said, "Enter ye in at the strait gate: for wide is the gate, and broad is the way, that leadeth to destruction, and many there be which go in thereat: because strait is the gate, and narrow is the way, which leadeth unto life, and few there be that find it" (7:13,14). He evidently did not think all roads go the same way or lead to the same place. He gives another picture of the same truth in verses 24-27: "Whosoever heareth these sayings of mine, and doeth them, I will liken him unto a wise man, which built his house upon a rock: and the rain descended, and the floods came, and the winds blew, and beat upon that house; and it fell not: for it was founded upon a rock. And every one that heareth these sayings of mine, and doeth them not, shall be likened unto a foolish man, which built his house upon the sand: and the rain descended, and the floods came, and the winds blew, and beat upon that house; and it fell: and great was the fall of it."

Jesus said something very important when He said, "Except ye be converted, and become as little children" (18:3). We human beings are a stubborn race. We are known for our rebellion. We need that childlike quality of humility if we are to change direction. It is hard for us to admit our failures, our sin and our need. We cling to anything which will allow us to continue in our own way. We comfort our hearts with little sayings about how we are "day by day in every way getting better and better." Are we? In what way? History tells us we have created nothing but havoc with everything we have touched. The Scriptures testify that we lack the power to change our direction as surely as the leopard lacks the power to change its spots (see Jer. 13:23). And current events would not give you the idea that we are about to sprout wings, grow halos over our heads and live like the proverbial angel!

The thing we likely do not realize is that the direction we take also determines the direction of the heart, the life, the behavior. God not only wants us to change direction so we will end up in the right place; He wants us to change character so we will act right while we go the right way. No wonder wise Solomon wrote: "Ponder the path of thy feet, and let all thy ways be established. Turn not to the right hand nor to the left: remove thy foot from evil" (Prov. 4:26,27).

Ponder the path of our feet. What direction are we going? What appears at the end of the road? If we are going the wrong direction, what can we expect at the end of the journey? Any man, trying to get home, would not be so foolish as to keep going in the wrong direction once he knew the right one. It is not too difficult to determine our destination. "The path of the just is as the shining light, that shineth more and more unto the perfect day. The way of the wicked is as darkness" (vv. 18,19). Ponder the path. Is there light at the end of the journey? Ponder, and "mark the perfect man, and behold the upright: for the end of that man is peace" (Ps. 37:37).

No wonder Asaph sang with broken heart to the "Shepherd of Israel" (Ps. 80:1), "Turn us again, O God, and cause thy face to shine; and we shall be saved" (v. 3). Psalm 85:3,4 says, "Thou hast taken away all thy wrath: thou hast turned thyself from the fierceness of thine anger. Turn us, O God of our salvation, and cause thine anger toward us to cease."

When the early Christians were scattered from Jerusalem and were preaching, "the hand of the Lord was with them: and a great number believed, and turned unto the Lord" (Acts 11:21). Paul, in presenting his case before King Agrippa, said he was following a heavenly vision in which he was told to go to the Gentiles "to open their eyes, and to turn them from darkness to light, and from the power of Satan unto God, that they may receive forgiveness of sins, and inheritance among them which are sanctified by faith" (26:18).

Homer was right when he said, "No man or woman born, coward or brave, can shun his destiny." While we cannot shun it, we can choose it. The wise man ponders his path and, finding himself on the wrong road, going in the wrong direction, turns about, takes a new road, another direction, a new Lord.

Chapter 10

A Poor Concept of the Delights of the Lord

My father used to say that a man has just collected enough wisdom and common sense to begin to live when it is time to die. Passing on to others our wisdom and those things which assure us of blessings in life has always been a problem. We cannot understand why others cannot see what we see. When we do discover some new knowledge, experience or blessing, we say, "Why was I blind so long?" Is not our lack of accepting all the Lord has for us a result of not seeing the delights of the Lord? Does not our blindness rob us of many blessings? The Devil has tried every trick and every temptation and has used every deception and lie on us in order to deceive us concerning the delights of surrender to the Lord. As a result we are like kings' sons who never know their heritage.

There is enough here to give the serious seeker pause for thought. Much of what he has seen in the lives of those who claim to be followers of the Lord does not speak of joy. He has seen fraud and hypocrisy. He has heard the disgruntled disciples as they have complained about everything around them. They complain of the restrictions under which they think they labor as followers of the Lord. They are never quite happy with the weather; they are upset concerning politics, though they seldom offer a hand to help. They decry the conditions of the church and complain that it certainly is not feeding the people. They criticize the preacher—he is either too liberal or too evangelical. They run down their neighbors and are purely and simply bitter.

When the poor soul who is considering his need for the Lord sees himself in his mind's eye turning out like that, it is no wonder he turns sadly away. If that is what it means to follow the Lord, then he does not want that—nor do we! He has no way of knowing that many who profess to follow the Lord never really follow Him and never seriously intended to do so. He has no way of knowing that some are babes in Christ and must be trained and taught before they will be mature and able to practice what they preach. He has reason for hesitation in his decision to follow the Lord.

Then, too, he has to contend with all the things he has learned from hearsay—and you can learn a lot of strange and wonderful things from hearsay! Every one of us can be glad we do not have to meet God on the grounds of the things people have said about us. Someone is always repeating a story they have heard about a preacher or a congregation which casts a bad light. Of course, things happen that should not happen, but the chances are the story as told is a million miles from the facts.

> Little rumor, running round,
>   Dying to be heard!

Gossip, lingering near the sound,
  Added on about one-third!

But gossip's friends, hearing the word,
  And not knowing all the facts,
Added on still another third,
  So black would still be black!

And so the little rumor,
  Which hardly meant a thing,
When it was full grown
  Had *killed* a mighty king!

No wonder those who have no way of knowing or understanding what a real Christian is have a perverted sense of all that goes under the name of Christ. They feel a Christian is one who is totally without the joy of living. He has simply missed it all. The poor fellow, this follower of the Lord, must be content to be bored if he is to be blessed. He must not smile, lest he crack his pious veneer. He is chained to a narrow life, charged with unnatural sobriety, excluded from everything pleasurable and denied the right to breathe freely.

It is nearly impossible for some to believe that the truth is exactly the opposite. Nehemiah said, "For the joy of the Lord is your strength" (Neh. 8:10), and that was in Old Testament times. "The fruit of the Spirit is . . . joy" (Gal. 5:22), which is to say that one thing the Holy Spirit will certainly produce in the life He controls is joy. "The kingdom of God," said the Apostle Paul, "is not meat and drink; but righteousness, and peace, and joy in the Holy Ghost" (Rom. 14:17). Jesus said, "And ye shall know the truth, and the truth shall make you free" (John 8:32), and "These things have I spoken unto you, that my joy might remain in you, and that your joy might be full" (15:11).

Fenelon said, "Happy the soul which, by sincere self-renunciation, holds itself ceaselessly in the hands of its Creator, ready to do everything which He wishes; which never stops saying to itself a hundred times a day, 'Lord, what wouldst thou that I should do? Teach me to perform thy holy will, for thou art my God. Thou wilt show that thou art my God by teaching me, and I will show that I am thy creature by obeying thee. In whose hands, great God, should I be better off than in thine?'" (*Christian Perfection*, p. 4). "We only want to do what we are doing, and we do not want to do anything at all which we are not doing" (p. 35). If we knew the delights of the kingdom of God, the courts of the King would be crowded.

It follows naturally that if one does not know what a real Christian is, he does not know what the church is for. His idea of the church is a place where the preacher scolds you for wrongdoing. Or his idea is that the church is a place for the people who feel they are just a bit better than the people who do not attend. The church is, therefore, he thinks, full of hypocrites who nod politely to God one day a week and do as they please just as soon as they are out of the church building. Any thinking person should know that just going into a building will not change a person.

Billy Sunday is quoted as saying, "If going into a church will make you a Christian, then going into a barn will turn you into a horse." One is as true as the other. No, the so-called church cannot change a person. The work of the Church as it meets together is to teach the Word of God. As the Word

88

of God is preached and taught, it acts as a check on our lives (Heb. 4:12). The Church is to inspire to good works (3:13; 10:24), to worship God (10:22; John 9:31; Phil. 3:3) and to bear one another's burdens (Gal. 6:1,2; I Thess. 5:14).

The Church, when it leaves the building (for the building is not the Church) is to live honest, godly, well-balanced and joyful lives (Titus 2:11-13) and is to be a witness to the death and resurrection of Jesus Christ (Acts 2:32) and the faithfulness and grace of God (Matt. 28:19; Acts 1:8; 26:22).

"In the third persecution Pliny the Second, a man learned and famous, seeing the lamentable slaughter of Christians, and moved therewith to pity, wrote to Trajan, certifying him that there were many thousands of them daily put to death, of which none did any thing contrary to the Roman laws worthy persecution. 'The whole account they gave of their crime or error (whichever it is to be called) amounted only to this—viz. that they were accustomed on a stated day to meet before daylight, and to repeat together a set form of prayer to Christ as a God, and to bind themselves by an obligation—not indeed to commit wickedness; but, on the contrary—never to commit theft, robbery, or adultery, never to falsify their word, never to defraud any man: after which it was their custom to separate, and reassemble to partake in common of a harmless meal' " (*Fox's Book of Martyrs*, p. 7). As false rumors went out then, they still go out, and many were and are cheated of the delights they could and should have enjoyed.

If a person has little real understanding of what a Christian is or what the church is for, he is not likely to understand the role of the minister. In the minds of many, the minister may be anything from a sort of lord over his flock to the laughingstock of society—from the sublime to the ridiculous.

A minister, to some, must be a man raised somewhere away from the real world of men. He certainly never knew temptation, never really walked in the everyday dirt and dust like other men. A lady, talking with me about her minister, once said, "I just don't believe he ever did anything wrong in his life!" She was a little upset when I suggested they had better get rid of him and get someone who knew he was a sinner like everybody else and who had tasted of the great grace of God, because he was going to have to minister to people who had sinned and who needed someone who could explain the grace of God to them.

To most, the preacher is a little unmanly, a weakling, a Milquetoast, someone who needs a big brother to take care of him. Did you ever see a play or a cartoon where the preacher, the parson or the reverend was not some sort of weirdo? He is never quite normal, never real, never fully sincere or trustworthy.

I know more preachers than the average man knows. Of course there are some phonies, but if I had to choose one group with which I had to live forever, I would take the preachers, hands down. This is to take nothing away from anyone else, but most ministers are a million miles from the twisted concept the average person has of them.

The great tragedy, however, for the man who does not seek God is that he has no idea of who Christ is, of what He has done and of what He can do in the heart of a man. He rebels because he simply does not know the delights which God has for the redeemed.

The whole Bible was written so that we may know redemption and salvation. There is personal assurance of salvation when trust is placed in the Saviour (I John 5:11-13). There is forgiveness of sins (Eph. 1:7), and there is justification before God (Rom. 4:25). There is the joy of knowing that life is not just a duty to perform but a delight, a pleasure (I Pet. 1:8). There is the unsearchable and rich truth that the Christian life is not the best I can do but is Christ coming to live His life in me (Col. 1:27). There is release from the fear of death (Heb. 2:14-18) and the knowledge that we are on our way to an eternal home (John 14:1-6).

Let no man think lightly of these things; they are the answers to the deepest longings of our souls. We often laugh them off because we do not know how to obtain them, but it is no laughing matter. Not too many things, or people, in this world are friends of grace and will help us on to God. Not many are displaying the delights of being a real child of God, but the delights are real nevertheless, and they are reachable. The sincere, seeking soul should have no trouble finding reality.

Jesus said, "Come unto me, all ye that labour and are heavy laden, and I will give you rest. Take my yoke upon you, and learn of me; for I am meek and lowly in heart: and ye shall find rest unto your souls. For my yoke is easy, and my burden is light" (Matt. 11:28-30). Revelation 22:17 says, "Whosoever will, let him take the water of life freely." Is the man who goes his own way and risks eternity a wise man? If somehow we could know the delights of a life surrendered to the Lord, it would make all the difference in this world and even in the next world. No man need fear surrendering completely to the Lord. It will be just as David said: "He shall give thee the desires of thine heart" (Ps. 37:4).